sack nasty

prison

poetry

by

ra avis

cover illustration

by

erik buikema

Copyright © 2016 by Ra Avis
All rights reserved.

No part of this publication may be reproduced, distributed, or transmitted in any form or by any means, including photocopying, recording, or other electronic or mechanical methods, without the prior written permission of the publisher, except in the case of brief quotations embodied in critical reviews and certain other noncommercial uses permitted by copyright law.

ISBN-13 978-1945681042

Printed in the United States of America

Cover Credits:
Erik Buikema
www.ErikBuikema.com

Ordering Information:
Quantity sales. Special discounts are available on quantity purchases by corporations, associations, and others. For details, contact the publisher.

Hostile 17 Print
www.hostile17print.com

Dedicated to Dave

He said freedom sustains itself,
so I shouldn't eat the lies they feed me;
That my hungry time would be full again,
and not to let them bleed me.
He made sure I was lovingly nourished
every moment I was locked away—
and promised no matter the obstacle,
he'd always find a way.

and to my Best Beloveds…
for always being the way.

The Prison Timeline

In May of 2014, a warrant was filed for Ra's arrest. She was charged with 247 felonies related to white collar crimes, and she surrendered herself to a police station where she spent the first day of her incarceration. She was then taken to Orange County Jail where she spent almost four months attempting to sign a plea deal with the help of a public defender. In August, she was shipped to the Central California Women's Facility in Chowchilla, where she spent just over three months— the first chunk on A-Yard, the second on D-Yard. She was then transferred to the California Institute for Women in Chino Hills where she spent four months in the FireCamp training area, colloquially called RIC. She failed the FireCamp program and was sent to a different unit to work as a structure firefighter for the prison firehouse. She was released on July 18th, 2015. On July 18th, 2016, she will be off of parole and finally, truly, free.

Table of Contents

Hard Time

They say she is property.
They say the world is better without her.
She absorbs it all.

Leashed by time, she makes the motions of the
living— fully invested in the moment—
knowing there is pain any other way.
Each step forward must be taken without a
backwards glance—
or the collar pulls
and the seconds solidify.
She wants malleable minutes.
Liquid hours.
She never wanted to experience hard time.

The caged shell cannot hold in her seeping,
melting soul. It is escaping—
leaving her empty, but emotionally free.
From the outside, she is.
On the inside, she merely was.

Sack Nasty

The deputy props a box
on her knee
while she unlocks the door,
entering the cell
baton first.
The box contents are thrown on the floor,
and she backs out of the room,
shouting “Stay back” on repeat,
as if anyone had moved.

Once the door closes, she kicks it.
She shouts, “goddamn animals.”
and she and her fellow badges laugh.

It’s the first food I’ve seen since jailed,
twelve hours ago.
But the girls warn me to eat with caution.

We call the brown bags and the content in them a
Sack Nasty.

And we never trust
what they feed us.

Not the food,
And never,
never,

the lies.

No Words

On A-Yard— prison receiving— the library was closed to us.

I sold a bag a coffee for a Koontz book and first dibs on a story about a raccoon. It was my only bag of coffee for the month. The women in my room traded lunches for book dibs. There was no library access, and the books sent our way were held back for months in the shipping room, often not arriving till we left.

I stopped a correctional officer, one of my favorites, from throwing away a book that was left outside after an emergency lockdown.

Tears ran down my face, and he paused. “There are pages missing,” he explained as he lifted it out of the trash, and I thought that I must look like a beggar to him.

I thought of the stories I heard growing up, about children stealing the wrappers of candy bars from the trashcans of tourist-trap hotels so they could lick the chocolate residue up. I thought of the people lying under stained blankets because any warmth was better than none on a cold night in the streets of LA. In that moment, it doesn't matter what it looks like to anyone else, or even yourself on a different day. I reached out, and the book that smelled like trash, with pages missing, was placed in my hands. I took it immediately back to my room where my cellmates and I read through it time and time again.

Later that week, I met a staff member who lent me a copy of *The New Yorker*, September 2014, and I read every word in there until it was memorized, and then again. Many days, it was the only thing I was able to read, and certainly it was one of the few writings that could mentally engage me, at the level to which I was accustomed..

Our room was tossed one day — slang for when the officers come through and shuffle everything around looking for contraband. The mattresses were on the ground, our clothes knocked everywhere, but *The New Yorker* was set carefully to the side, because everyone knows how precious something like that is, in a place like that. Even officers.

It is chocolate, to a starving belly, it is a cashmere blanket on the streets of a city forgotten by everyone but the cold. It is luxury and deepest need.

There's a shortage of books, always, even as you proceed forward— even as the experience gets better— and the breadth covered in those books is limited.

We're cold there, sometimes— hungry, often— and questing for knowledge and the warmth of human wordings, always.

It wasn't just me, it was my 65-year-old white bunky with a 3rd grade education, and my 32-year-old black transgender friend who loved her Honda, and that daughter of a Navy captain, and the teenage mom with a cat named Seaweed, and the girl who saw her husband murdered months before being arrested, and everyone. *Everyone.*

Just because we didn't have an opportunity to expand our minds, doesn't mean there wasn't a want.

I understand the confusion because it's easy to see the outcome. Some women have spent years learning not to let those tears fall, not even for deepest need. Some women don't have my superpower of finding the best of people everywhere. Some women don't have family out here that can send money for them to buy coffee that they can trade for the most coveted possessions.

What you see as a "normal inmate" is a result, and you're assuming a causation, and the intent behind that causation.

And you are wrong.

You don't know, you didn't know, and maybe— maybe— you couldn't have known.

But now you do.

I was a normal inmate, but I had an abnormally wondrous network outside, and that accounts for most of the differences you can see with your naked eye. From where you are standing, the gates outside that place can't be seen, and certainly can't be smelled or tasted. I am doing my best to stand where you are, to wash the taste of cuffs and barriers from my life— but while I still wear the shackles, mental if not physical, I want to use the clarity to shine a little light for you.

There's a vacuum in prisons and it tries to suck down the quest for Better. There's a shortage of words and it eats Hope.

But we come home anyway.

Maybe it doesn't look like we tried there, because we were so busy surviving there, but as someone who lived inside those gates— let me assure you—

We tried. All of us. Even when there were no words.

Words are magical, and as rare as magic inside the cage. There's a lack of substance, not a lack of want.

I was luckier, not better, and it's important you know that because we— those of us walking in freedom— can do better, but we won't if we keep pretending that we know the women who are in there. We won't if we keep pretending that we know what their punishment is, or what is right and fair and productive in the pursuance of that punishment.

All we know is what we see, from our very safe distance away.

So sit next to me, and let me tell you what I saw there, while I still see it oh-so-clearly.

Listen, to the words I say, and all the things I can't. Listen to the spaces where there should have been magic, where there could have been stories. Let me give you some of the characters that take up so much space in my heart, so you can mix in your gut responses and brilliant thoughts. Let's start a story that takes us through all the things we still need to know.

So maybe we can know more and do better… no matter where we live, relative to the cage.

Of Ladies and Fools

Nobody wanted to be inside tonight.

The moon was blood-red, the stars were silent, and the sky was black. We couldn't see the barbed wire gates that surrounded us. We couldn't hear the clanging of keys, or the shouting of guards. We couldn't feel the dark blue khaki uniforms, made for men, folding awkwardly around us.

If we wanted to, we could fool ourselves into thinking we were free, and we wanted to.

I was walking with Tammy. She strutted alongside my amble, her chin held high—femininity pouring from every curve in her form. "Which direction?" she asked me, her fingertips lightly brushing my arm. I smiled. She had a way of making our days feel like they were rife with choice.

In reality, we only had a yard the size of a small football field. There was an oval pathway and three concrete benches on the grass inside the oval. We shared this yard with the other inmates housed on D-Yard of Central California Women's Facility — the largest female correctional facility in the United States. There were probably 500 of us on D-Yard, and it seemed like almost all of us were out that night.

I pointed, and we began to walk.

… Past the couple who were married on the yard yesterday— *they'll never last*, Tammy said.

… Past my old cellmate who enthusiastically waved— *Her mama stops sending her money finally, and all'a sudden she's got waves*, Tammy smirked.

… Past a old woman who blew me a kiss— *Don't you dare Rara-her and treat her like she's normal*, Tammy warned, *do you know what that heffer is here for?*

Tammy was here for stabbing a man. Like every woman incarcerated and sentenced to a state prison term— like me— she was sent to CCWF's receiving yard to be processed. The girls call it A-Yard. She was the last inmate checked into the prison on a Friday. I was the first checked in on a Monday and so, though we didn't meet till a month later, our prison ID numbers were only one digit off. Friendships have been formed on less.

On A-Yard, we worked together. I was a clerk and she was the game girl, so we would prepare the dayroom for the other girls during their hour of freedom a day. Between the two of us, and our social-butterfly ways, we knew every woman who came into CCWF over the course of four months. We both ran a tight schedule, which was unique— for most women, A-Yard is prison purgatory. Until you are transported elsewhere, you are locked in a room all day long, unless they are testing you for something.

Most girls sleep the days away, hoping to go to a smaller facility. CCWF is not where you want to stay.

Unlike the smaller prisons that may accept you after you complete the receiving process, CCWF is an all-levels prison. This means it houses all kinds; the woman who repeatedly steals shampoo, the woman who poisoned an abusive husband, the woman who set herself on fire in a public place, and the woman on death row. When you leave receiving and go to one of the main sections— called going "over the wall"— the sort of women you will be around is anyone's guess.

The A-Yard prayer is simple. Send me away quickly— anywhere except over the wall.

When Tammy and I got the call to go to D-Yard— we linked hands, and walked out together in the state-issued blue polka-dotted muumuus. We weren't worried about staying. We were rollover. They were sending us over the wall so they could move us elsewhere. Tammy was destined for a smaller working prison and I was headed to the FireCamp program at the California Institute for Women. We walked from A-Yard to D-Yard, with 25 other inmates, carrying all our belongings on our back, in nylon mesh bags.

Somehow, despite the uneven gravel under our flip-flopped feet and the heaviness of our bags and hearts, Tammy still sauntered. I was grateful just to not fall on my face.

A few of the women caught up to me, to ask if

this was legal— this method of moving us from one place to another, just to make room. Tammy shooed them away and I let her.

The truth is, it didn't matter.

What would any of us do if it wasn't?

The only thing in our power was walking forward and being grateful, even though we were destined to go the long way.

And, tonight, I had plenty to be grateful for, even here on D-Yard.

The moon was big and I could be outside to see it. In county jail, I went four months without seeing the sky at night. Just over the wall, back on A-Yard, were a few staff members I trusted entirely with my welfare. I knew I wasn't staying in this place. Eventually, someone would make sure that I was moved somewhere better.

Not that it was all miserable here. I wasn't a total misfit. I knew almost all the girls on this yard and they knew me. I felt safe among them, and loved.

Tammy's comforting humming, and my thoughts, were interrupted by a blaring

announcement over the speakerphone.
YARD DOWN YARD DOWN, ALL INMATES DOWN.

There was a collective groan. In the night, we looked around for whatever trouble-maker caused this newest interruption to our moment of near-freedom. The grass was wet, and none of us wanted to sit on it.

"Yard Down, ladies," the officers shouted as they ran past us, towards the commotion.

We sat.

"This yard stays down," Tammy muttered unhappily. The lights flickered and the yard went dark. There were shuffling sounds and then screaming. From behind us, there was a spark of light and the sound of a pepper gun being shot. Tammy pulled my arm, tugging me backwards, so that my back was to the wall. Then she scooted until she was in front of me. *Just in case*, she said.

All around us there were bursts of light, as non-lethal firearms were deployed, and as flashlights flailed about in the center. We heard keys and handcuffs, screaming, and then silence. Then more silence.

The Yard went completely dark, until one light blinked slowly to life, just in front of me. It illuminated a bright pink traffic cone. I hadn't noticed on our first walk around, but I saw it clearly now— a vibrant, beautiful magenta I hadn't seen in months.

"Oh, what a gorgeous traffic cone!" I exclaimed.

In the stillness, my voice carried and filled the yard. Tammy turned to look at me, one perfect eyebrow, wildly arched.

There was a second more of a silence, and then from hundreds of feet away, I heard a responding voice.

"Fucking Rara."

Everyone laughed— hundreds of women who had met me before, sitting on the wet grass on a dark night, laughing because the way I didn't fit in had become our inside joke. And because we could.

We weren't walking off the yard and going home, but we weren't the ones walking off the yard with our wrists trapped in cold metal, headed toward jail-jail either. We weren't the ones shot with a pepper gun that night. It was something to find relief in, some place to find joy. Somethin' to do.

YARD IS UP AND YARD IS CLOSED. The speakerphone blared its announcement and there was a collective groan.

The grass was wet, but at least we were outside. "This yard stays closed," Tammy grumbled. "Should we walk directly back or go the long way?"

I smiled. The stars were so silent we could hear all our choices. The chilled night was so dark, we shivered with freedom.

We had to go in, but not just yet.

"Let's go the long way," I replied.

"Gurl," Tammy agreed with her trademark purr. "The long way is the only way we know."

She sauntered forward. I ambled beside her. The blood moon followed us and her soft hum led the way. In the darkness, we could fool ourselves into thinking we were free.

So we happily played the fool.

Flushed

In county jail, the toilets flush hard,
hard enough to leave a bruise behind you
if you're too slow.

I was too slow, once.
But I learned to be fast.
I learned to think faster.

Hurry up, they all say there,
Hurry up,
and wait.
I waited to use the bathroom
for 20 hours after my wrists were first cuffed.
I sat on thoughts
instead of a throne,
and stewed.
Less than a year later, I made stew
in a trash bag
stored it in a toilet we emptied,
after we borrowed the toilet brush.

The toilet brush.

One brush for a hundred and twenty girls
and no cleaning chemicals,
because we're beyond sanitizing
We're all diseased waste
according to the papers.

So we did what we could—
scrubbed,
emptied,
and filled the negative space
with something heartening.

The girls in another county empty their toilets
all the time,
as they do time.
They're housed on the 2nd floor,
and the boys are housed below.
If you empty the toilets,
you can talk through them.
Flirt through them.
Promise through them.

They get through their trials that way,

preferring a place to put their love
over a place to put their
waste.

There's so much waste.
We flush it all.

Contraband flowers made from toilet paper
and yesterday's news,
flush it.
Flush it.

That extra bra, the cigarettes you made
from tea and strips of the Bible.
Flush it.

Flush it down.

The girls perch on top,
sliding their fingers into themselves
to remove drugs smuggled in.

They reach inside
and pull a new reality
off their shelf.

It isn't a euphemism,
It's a you and me issue,
it's a sanitation issue,
and a damn waste.

There's so much waste.
Flush it down.

We're locked up,
sometimes for days in a cell.
In prison, the toilets flush once,
then once again,
then not again for minutes.
The first is for courtesy,
the second to finish,
but if you time it wrong,
you and your bunky choke on the smell.
The toilets are three feet from the bunk
where her face rests.

The flush will wake her up at night,
and she will see inside you
every time you wipe yourself clean.
But you have to wipe anyway.
There's so much waste.

In county, they turned off the water,
without telling us.
Why would they? We just lived there.
My bunky then, 8 months pregnant,
held what she could till I caught on.
"Go", I said,
and she did,
over and over through the day
like healthy pregnant women do.
But the smell made her sick
and no food stayed down.

The toilet started to flush wildly
at night,
when the water turned back on,
and I was startled off my bunk,
and chipped a tooth.

I cleaned chipped toilets,
and toilets used by fire captains,
and toilets used by life-long hookers,
and almost all of them without gloves
because I was part of the waste.

I was flushed.

I begged for toilet paper,
and was strip searched after promising
that my room had none.

The woman in the cell next to me ate hers,
I suspect,

and when the badges stopped giving her any,
I would smuggle the sheets through her door,
and her eyes would fill with tears
of gratitude.
She wasn't a kind person (yet),
but I never believed she was waste, either,
no matter what they said.

You don't flush people,
you flush things.

I flushed a toothpaste tube
full of cocaine,
several dozen apple cores,
and—
on the day they told me
I was a widow—

on the day they told me
he ran out of time while I was doing time,
I flushed everything I had written
since those cuffs
first touched my wrists.

To go to his funeral I stood over a community
prison toilet and peed,
a woman I had met that morning
watching the stream land
in a tiny plastic container.

She taped it up
and wrote my name on it.
Not the one that goes back
uncounted generations,
but the one that is nothing but a count
WF0124.
What a waste.
I held it all in,
and left it all behind,
but opened my eyes
so I could see the marks it left.

There's so much waste,

so

much

waste.
All of it bruises,
and only some of it
flushes.

Lupe Snores

She reminds me of mama, a Latina fairy godmother—
tough eyes, soft skin, catchphrases no one can spell.
I go over the wall with her, both of us in muumuus, and she says
I look *tan bonita* in polka dots.
I roll my eyes, and she pinches my chin like mama does.
I wonder why she is here, how she will fare.
Lupe has a family out there, I pray she returns.
We fall asleep cuddled, waiting for cells.
I dream.
Lupe snores.

The word is one of my girls is being bullied,
lifers attacking unclassified muumuus like me.
I read the dayroom faces for words we can't say—
all of us just want to make it out of here.

Lupe has bags under her eyes and tears in them.
She's not allowed to sleep in her room 'cos
Lupe snores.

We leave handcuffed together, to a kinder cage.
Not even the shotgun at our backs stops our joy
when the smog fills the air
and traffic blocks our path.
These are our skies, roads— our families are here.
I dislocate my shoulder so our linked cuffs don't
cut her skin.
She doesn't notice 'cos she's humming for me.
It's like mama's sound, and I pray she makes it
home
so her daughter can hear her, and she'll surely
hear her 'cos
Lupe snores.

Nuts

The officer
dropped a packet of pistachios
in the trash and
winked at me,

but I did not retrieve it
because I would never
pay that much
for a nut.

Braids

Only the black girls
can have more than two braids.

Her girlfriend on the inside was black
so she thought she was the exception.
She wore her hair in four,

and they cupped her—

taking a plastic mug
and slamming it into her body
repeatedly.

She broke her wrist,
lost her sight in one eye,
and swore the whole time
it was because
she slipped
on shampoo.

Sweet Rot

I was raised in a town the size of a thimble,
surrounded by small dreams and big freedoms,
and the nation's finest apple orchards.
But even the best apples taste rotten to me,
rotten to the seedy core.
There, cores outnumber beating hearts
10,000 to 1
and I didn't like those odds,
or those apples,
so I left.

. . .

Years later, I went to prison full of big dreams
that landed people in small rooms,
smaller than a knot on a thimble,
where nothing grows, least of all people.
There, they fed us an apple a day,
which might have been their seedy justification
for keeping the doctors away.

I didn’t like those apples either
so I didn’t eat
till the hunger became so powerful it disappeared
and all I felt was bone-weary weakness.

. . .

It was a 60-year-old street hooker
who finally convinced me to eat one,
reminding me: the air is often rotten,
and the system is always rotten, but
we still have to breathe. To survive.
Eat the rot or be the rot, she said,
and I listened.
I ate. I ate while I prayed
that the rot wouldn’t get my core.

. . .

So my heart keeps beating.
The beats outnumbering lost dreams and
freedoms, 10,000 to 1.

I like my odds.

And I like the apples I bite into in freedom
because they taste rotten.

And some days
that's the only way
I know
that any part of me
survived.

Snitches

Snitches get stitches, they say,
knowing full well
that *no one* gets stitches.
The prison doctors issue only
pregnancy tests,
no matter your ailment.
But nothing is born in prison
more than baseless
accusations
and rumors.
There's no test for truth,
and no stitches for the daughters
who bleed out on a yard
on the basis of what they said
they said.
Snitches get stitches, they say,
and that lullaby of justification
soothes the lies we tell ourselves
about the necessity
of punishment.

5150

She sang Amazing Grace at 3am
during chow time.
My cell was stacked on top of hers,
a little to the right.

I couldn't see her,
but I heard her.
Everyone did.

Something about the way she sang
made bumps rise over my skin.
Maybe it was how loudly she was singing.
Maybe it was that
she
just
didn't
stop.

It was 5am and she was still singing.

The deputies were trying
to reason with her now.

Come on out, they said,
but she didn't.

She didn't stop.
She sang louder.

Louder and louder.

Step free, they commanded,
but you can't command someone
who is so free
that they no longer exist
on your plane.

I couldn't see her,
but I heard her.
Every hair on my body
was listening to her song.
Eventually they sent more deputies,
and more,

till the room was filled with badges,
so she took her clothes off,
screaming,
throwing them through the door—

throwing everything through the door.

She took the last sheet from the bed,
and stood on the toilet,

still roaring
her anthem
like an angry lioness.

I couldn't see her,
but they announced the progress,
recording everything,
to prove action was required,
for her own safety,

and certainly not just
to stop the agonizing sound.

Finally, the deputies called 5150.
I could see them coming.

A team of eight large men
in SWAT gear and shields
who raced toward her room
at full speed.

She charged them,
a 5-foot-nothing ball of naked fury,
running into my full view,

so they slammed her
face down onto a gurney.

Where she kept screaming
as they strapped her down,
and kept singing
as they covered her face,
and kept roaring
as they wheeled her away.

They said she was crazy,

and needed to be 5150'd,
because — look—
she charged the men.

but I could only think
that if eight men charged me
with batons out and armor on,
pedigree or sanity aside,
nudity notwithstanding,
I'd give myself
my best shot, too.

What they didn't seem to grasp
no matter how loudly she sang,
is how preciously she believed—
That Grace had brought her safe thus far
and Grace
would
lead
her
home.

Home became a cell to herself,
where they took away her clothes,
suggesting she sing
for therapy,

never considering the irony
of solving a problem
they created

using the solution
that they saw as
the original problem.

Amazing Grace,
how sweet your sound.

I was blind,
but now

I see.

EOP

EOP is a program for the incarcerated girls
who need a little extra care.
On the Yard, they're called the crazies,
but it's illegal to be mentally ill in this country,
so they're filed along
arsonists and car thieves alike.

Before they are sorted,
they are housed in general population.

They are taken off their medications,
because drugs aren't worth the cost of sanity.
Because sanity isn't a right in this country,
and only *rights* are subsidized by
the state.

My friend, taken off the psych meds
she'd taken religiously for 8 years,
woke at night
to sniff my clean panties

and fold my dirty towel,
over and over again.

Another used my toothbrush
to wipe herself clean.

Another cried
into my arms all night
because none of her words
came out right,
and she didn't understand
why.

Most of the other girls
didn't understand either.

Mental illness is not something we learn about
in this country,
it is something we want to forget
like the thousands
and thousands of women
we lock away.

No More Kisses

Did you know we
jail our veterans
for being homeless?

I did not.

I didn't know
when I was a little girl in San Antonio
blowing kisses at the planes
that my dad said were carrying our heroes
home.

Just like I didn't know,
at the time,
that those planes I saw sometimes carried
coffins.

I didn't know we took people,
taught them to be removed from society,
to protect us,

and then punished them
for being removed
from society.

I didn't know.

I didn't know that
when they end up in jail,
they're penalized for their skill.
Forbidden from the few rehabilitation programs
where they might know enough
to know too much.

I didn't know that when I was a eighteen,
either,
as I blew kisses to my classmates
who were going to be
archaeologists, doctors,
teachers, lawyers,
when they got back.
If
they got back.

I was raised to believe
our troops were heroes
because they sacrificed for
the collective mind—
gave up their homes
because we needed them
to be homeless,
unbound to land,
mobile.

I didn't know
we only counted them
as heroes
when we needed them.

I didn't know we jailed them
for the sacrifices
we taught them
to make.

I didn't know,
and now I wonder how many
heroes were suffering

while I was blowing kisses

at the marketing posters

that landed them

a longer sentence

than

mine.

Flunking

The black population
of California is 7%,
if you want to round up.

At least 25% of the women
who served time with me
were black,
if you want to round down.

I know not everyone
is comfortable with math,
or comfortable
on this
thought path,

or understands the implication
of numbers without faces,
or understands the effects
of incarcerating whole races,

and I know not everyone counts
dark skin as skin,

just as I know not everyone
thinks
everyone counts.

Not everyone thinks,
so I'll break it down,
explain the amounts.
In jail,
black women
represent almost four times
more than they should.

When equally represented
in punishment,
you can say the girls inside
failed the justice system,
failed us—
as a peoples
as a state.

But when a woman is more likely
to serve time because
of the color of her skin,
well,
that's the justice system
failing them.

That's us,
failing.

Not everyone is good at math,
but thanks to standardization of testing
in these united states,
I hope you all understand
that we're flunking
humanity,

because while
not everyone is good at math,
absolutely
every one
counts.

Knuckles

On Wednesday morning,
after breakfast,
some girls fought and
the Yard went down.
Looking for the perpetrators of violence,
the sergeant
held my hands in his,
examining them to ensure
they were not stained
with blood.

They weren't,
of course,
but it gave the possibility
to my imagination

and my knuckles have never looked
the same to me
since.

Mary Kay

When Mary Kay was coming down
you couldn't see the starlight in her eyes.
The green orbs were clouded,
shaking, darkened.
She hurt,
from the pain of heroin leaving her,
and the pain of all the things
she used heroin to hide.
When Mary Kay was coming down,
her body sweat,
even the tops of her feet,
and she thrashed and tangled her sheets,
and spoke words
she didn't mean.
She hurt, but I didn't
until she recovered enough
for me to understand
that some darkness
is too dark even for stars.

The Eleventh Day

The Yard had been closed to us,
for days.
Eleven little tally marks
on the lockers in our cells.

We peeked the sky
for only a moment
as we carried our resin mugs
and plastic spoons to chow.

It was Sunday when they announced
we could have one hour of access,
but the names of days matter so little
when they are not yours to have.

We walked past the scheduled church service,
not wanting to sacrifice
our hour in the sun,
not knowing when we'd have another.

The nun shouted
SHAME
as one by one we chose a moment in the light,
over the light in her book.

She thumped it—
and warned us to think of holy things
before making our decision.

It's in, she warned,
reminding us that we could not have both
freedom and grace.

In,
or out.

I chose out,
deciding
God was on the Yard,
too.

Maya

Maya Angelou died
while I was in county jail,
and the women I was with
didn't know her.

I read them her poems.
I told them her story.
Explaining her courage,
in the face of being
held back,
stepped on,
pushed aside,
Explaining
how she overcame it all.

One girl laughed
and said that made her
no different
than the rest of us,
or any woman.

I considered the thought
and decided it was because
she did something braver
than living her story.
She *told* her story.
Even to people who couldn't
understand just yet,
or maybe ever.

Like me, a reader who memorized her poems
in a classroom,
but never really heard them
till she died
while I was locked up.

Like me, a woman who spent a lifetime
solving the riddle of
why the caged bird sings
without ever wondering
how it finds the strength
to do so at all.

The Baton

The only time I ever saw him
need his baton
was when he snapped it open
to hold it against
my neck,

and ask
for a little
kiss.

Cells

They wouldn't stop fighting
about division.
Our cell was cold.

We had been waiting
for our court session.
My lawyer didn't show,
again,
but I would wait all day,
barefoot in a room
the temperature of a walk-in
cooler.

We all waited,
and after 4 hours of
being unfed and frozen,
someone in a suit
would slide over paperwork
and ask us to sign.

And usually we did,
because no one wanted
to do this again.

The cell was cold,
but they wouldn't stop fighting,
and I couldn't sleep
or think.

They had smuggled cocaine in a pad,
a miracle in itself
given that we have to
take off our pads
and ring them out
in front of the cops
who pat us down.

But they had smuggled cocaine,
and couldn't decide how
to split it three ways.

So I got up,
and did it for them,

and they made for me
a pillow of toilet paper,
so I could rest my head.

Later a cop said she was surprised
to see how friendly we all were.

She said it was magic,

And
I said most magic
was science.

In this case,
cell division.

Ice Cream

She was going through menopause
and the cells were so hot
that sometimes,
she could barely breathe.

I didn't eat the ice cream
so I thought I could take it back
to my cell,
in hopes that,
hours later,
it could cool her.

We're not allowed to take food
from the chowhall,
and I knew that,
but this was just a tiny
bit of ice cream.

On my way out,
the officer saw it

and made me throw it away,

where the ants

would get it,

and she

would

not.

Fire!

There was a fire in the prison,
and no one came.

My Captains called for back up,
but the city was busy,
probably.

We don't know because
they never returned that call.

The fire started in a giant
commercial
trash bin,
and no one outside the gates worried
Because — I'm guessing—
the worst it could do
was burn up
the human trash
inside.

My Captains stayed
till their legs gave out
and they were covered in soot
and our old fire engine
had not a damn
thing
left.

They stayed till the job was done.

We backed them up,
stone-faced and attentive,
justifying the time they spent training us.
Almost.

Hours later,
after wiping my engine down,
and rolling my hoses,
and washing the ash from our uniforms,
the reality hit and I cried.

Angry
angry tears.

No

one

even

called

us

back.

They didn't forsake us

because they were bad guys.

I wasn't crying

because they were bad guys.

I was crying because

every day,

it seemed like I was left

with less

and less

heroes.

A Misunderstanding

She took the drugs,
but couldn't pay.

The truth caught up to her
before she got to her cell
and they held her down,
reaching into every orifice,
searching.

Searching.

She had no time to hide the bags
or use the drugs.
There was no place
besides her body,
so they took a broken broom handle
and shoved it inside her
at every angle,
searching.

Searching.

The cops came then,
lamenting over the fragments
of vagina
all over the floor.

They took away broom access
from all inmates
for a week,
and it was around that time
when the drug dealers realized
they had searched
the wrong
girl.

Sock Locks

She left a piece of hair
on the toilet,
and a bologna wrapper on the floor,
and that's why they
beat her bloody with
a lock
in a sock.

It took two people
to hold her down,
while one slammed her,
because she fought back.

It took two people
to clean up her blood,
and three
to empty the mop bucket
filled to the brim
with bloodstained
water.

She left a piece of hair
on the toilet
and a bologna wrapper on the floor,
and anyone on the inside
who heard the beginning
of that story
knew exactly how it would end.

Our Warden

Our Warden was very funny.
She liked to play games.

Games like sitting with inmates
when Press was in town,
but locking them up for getting near her
when they weren't.
Games like starting a compassion fund
for inmates,
and then using the money
to close community areas
of the prison.

Our Warden was very funny.
She liked to tell jokes.

She told this one,
while wearing her best suit
about how she'd do the final hike
with the girls put in FireCamp.

The Press cheered because I guess
everyone can appreciate a joke
that's so funny it helps you forget
the blistered and broken limbs
of the girls pushed through
an involuntary work program.
A joke that’s so funny
it helps you forget that
indentured servitude still exists.

She also had this one about milestone credits,
and she’d tell Press that if we worked hard,
we could go home faster,
but really no classes for those credits
were offered.
That joke got us, every time.

Our Warden was very funny.
She had all kinds of quirks.

She liked our officers to count and restrict
how many feminine hygiene products
we were given in a month.

She liked our mail room girls
to send Valentine's Day cards back.

Our Warden was so very funny.
She had a great imagination.

She liked to pretend
no girls died inside the prison,
and if they did,
it certainly wasn't from a lack of required and
requested medical care.

She liked to pretend
no girls committed suicide,
and if they did,
it certainly wasn't a consequence of isolation
created by the closing of community areas.

She liked to pretend
we wouldn't notice,
the way fish don't notice
when you scoop a dead one
out.

Oh, our Warden.

She

Was

Very

Funny,

So funny,

I could have died.

The Slap

She said
    I said
        that she said
                they said
    that I said
she said.

It was about a boy,

It was about the linked ladders
that women forge.
A game we're taught,
where we connect ourselves together
but have to stay on top.

Links are bad architecture
when the goal is to outpace.
The game is rigged.
No one wins.

She said
    I said
        that she said
                they said
    that I said
she said.

We were playing Scrabble,
myself and one
of the shes.

That night on the Yard,
the world looked like we
had really put it through the ringer.
The ground was slightly damp,
The sky was slightly sagging.

The stars yawned
with every blink.

I walked with her, another she,
and she recapped for me.

She said
 I said
  that she said
    they said
 that I said
she said.

We were walking side by side,
and her arm shot out,
hitting my nose,
knocking me half a foot back.
Reminding me
to keep names outta my mouth.

I didn't hit back,
just asked if she was done,
and then walked back
to finish
the only type of game
I play.

Licks

A mama cat's instinct
to lick her kitten's wounds is the best available
medical treatment.
There's magic in mom—
a cure-most remedy embedded in her basic
building blocks.
Tonight I am wounded,
praying my nosebleed stops
and that bruises don't mar my face.
Thinking on cats,
I pile my mother's letters
onto my bunk bed and curl myself into them.
I sleep…
awakening only when my cell door is banged by
clanging keys.
Like an ointment,
her familiar scent clings to me
and my face is healed.
but the medicine doesn't work
on my caged heart.

This.

And yet despite
all the things I've seen,
the worst by far
is this:

Many of the girls
I met and knew,
are still
illiterate.

Handshakes

I extended my hand,
a habit from my early days
in Texas.

A meeting ends,
you leave the room,
your hand goes out
and the stranger squeezes it
and gives it a shake.

You can learn a lot
from a handshake.

The meeting ended,
I extended my hand,
and she shook her head.

"I don't shake the hands
of people in orange."
she said,

and I left her office,
with a nod of understanding.

An understanding of rehabilitation,
counseling, and how we hold
our truest beliefs
in our actions.

An understanding
of her,
and how grateful I was
that she'd remain
a stranger.

You can learn a lot
from a handshake.

Even one
that
doesn't
happen.

Accent

The good doctor said I
had an unusual accent
for this place.

I was born and raised
in this country,
this place,
and so I asked her
what accent she heard.

She thought for a moment,
then said,

"Educated.
You sound educated."

"That is the saddest thing I've ever heard,"
I said.

And for once, we both agreed.

Advice

"Keep walking.
Stop talking.
If they say they love you,
they want something.
If they say they're friends,
they're lying.
You can't trust them."

The deputy repeated this,
in a sing-song voice,
over and over again.

A reminder that inmates
should not trust inmates.

I laughed to myself
the first time I heard it,
knowing that I trust myself,
and I can be trusted.

Thus,
some of these women
can be trusted, too.

After 438 days incarcerated,
I met a woman going to prison
who asked for advice.

"Keep walking," I said.
"You can't trust them,
or anyone."

And as the words bubbled out,
I heard the sing-song
in my mind
and realized
somehow I had let it in
much farther
than I had ever
intended.

Clarity

Let me be clear:
I hate being a prisoner.
The very idea of it chafes my nature,
shakes my composure.
The reality of it torments me…
when I let it.

For you, I want to soften the blow
but — for me — for my survival here —
the tattered truth needs to remain.

Unpatched, unglittered.

Prison is what it is, and what it is, is ugly.
Every day.

It's the sort of deep-seated ugly
that goes back generations.
The sort of place built
on a forgotten moment of the universe—

a rotten house sinking into a divine blink.

It lives in an eternal state of near collapse,
a permanent pause in fragility's ode
to violence and cruelty.

But yes! —
it is splattered with soft beauties and rife with
miracles.
That is no exaggeration on my part.
True love flourishes here,
the North Star stays steadily faithful to each of its
misbegotten souls,
and the sun scares away yesterday's nightmares.

There is a good here, and it is frightful and
ferocious.

Still even the most precious of sparkles is simply
a diamond tacked to a sow's ear.
There's no pretending it is a silk purse.

And let me be clear — worse than being in prison
is being a prisoner.

Prison is just a place, even when it is hideous and
haunted.

Being a prisoner is a state of existence— a
sandpit of life that pulls dignity to your ankles,
undermines your rational mind,
litters your soul with sour faith,
and fills your mouth with sandy words.

All this is the truth.
But I try to hold it back from being my whole or
only truth.

I still celebrate here,
still savor each of my days.

I collect beauties, hunt gratitudes, and constantly
repaint the tear-worn shack walls.

I dig deep

into the sandpit to find the space where
— wildly and naturally—
joy blooms and trust grows.

I remind myself that you don't need a silk purse
to find happiness on the brink of a blink.

Most days, a sow's ear does just fine.

So I live my days, and rest my nights,
counting down to a time when my beloved
country will let me wear my tarnished humanity
again,

sending the fog in my soul up to the starlit sky
and the powers that light it.

Please, I pray.
Let me be clear.
Help
me
stay
clear.

Lifer

I went home,

but she

never

will.

She Don't Even Know

She wears a smile that chills.
It frosts my blood,
preparing me for flight
or fight.
She does not know
I could do both.

She wears a smile that chills.
She's happy to be here.
She does not know that I am happy, too.
Happy she's not with the ones
I love.
Or free, near the ones I raised.

She wears a smile till the door shuts,
and you get close enough
to see her teeth.

And then she whispers,
waiting for your eyes to fill with fear.

She wears a smile that chills.
I am sick when she is near me,
I am frozen when says my name.
She wanders her eyes
over my face,

She's smiling. She's sniffing.
She's looking for fear.

Her smile fades when
she cannot see it,
and I know my smile
is frosting her blood.

She doesn't understand
why someone as tame as I
does not crumple,
because she does not know

I grew up with
with wild animals.

Prison Break

I hurt myself
in the process of training
to be an inmate fire fighter.
I tore my hip.

Injury is a violation,
a refusal to program
when your program
depends on health.

I was penalized,
sent to the Yard,
to sit on a concrete bench
on the hottest day of the year.

My internal structure
is not made for prison,
so my bones rebelled.
Tearing through my skin.

There was nothing to do.
No one to call,
but in the delirium
of heat
and blood loss,

I found a sort of joy
in the idea
that some of me
was finally
free.

Lady Song

I stopped having periods
when I went to jail.

I was grateful.

I didn't want to bleed onto a sheet
that I had to sleep on
for another week.
I didn't want to strip out,
pulling down my panties,
while shoulder distance
from a stranger.

I was grateful.
I didn't want to beg for pads,
or make my own tampons.

I didn't want to be forced to sit
when I know my body
would resist.

I didn't want to have to walk
with clothes I bled through
or might have bled through,
and not know.
And not be allowed
to stop.

I stopped having periods
when I went to jail.

And I was grateful.

The doctors called me in,
to check,
and I told them of other girls
who had actual injuries
who had not been called.
But they were only concerned
with what was happening
between my legs.

They said it was the stress of new things,
but eventually jail became normal to me,

and still I did not start.

They said it was starvation,
but eventually I ate normally again,
and still I did not start.

They said it was hormones,
they said it was AIDS,
they said it was blood pressure,
and age.

They tested it all,
and found nothing,
but my inmate doctor
claimed she knew.

She said my body
missed my man.

She wasn't a doctor,
but her husband was,
and she made every flashcard and cheatsheet
that got him through school.

She wasn't a doctor,
but she was a woman
who had lived a lot of life.
More than most. More than me.

She said the doctors
couldn't test my lady song,
but that she could hear
the silence of my heart.

I didn't really believe her
till one year in,
when I finally got to hug my husband.
And as his arms
wrapped around me,
I could hear the song
where there had been silence,
and
I
finally
started
bleeding.

The Drip

Every minute of freedom is a sweet, slow-drip of syrupy goodness pouring through my veins.

As I drove away from the prison,
I felt the puncture.

The gates had barely shut behind me when the cold strength of the real world pieced through me. *You're back,* the Universe spoke in cool efficiency. *This will only sting for a second.*

No one understands seconds like someone who has watched them click by from a place that knows no time, like someone who has done time, and been done by time.

Every second of freedom is sugared and weighty. It solidifies in my bloodstream like little lemondrops. It is unquestionably sweet, miraculously tangy— and hard.

Heavy and hard.
On mornings like this, I miss prison.

The TV in the dayroom would be on KTLA, and we'd wait to be called for breakfast. We watched for Sam Rubin, the entertainment guy, so we could be outraged whenever he disagreed with our self-qualified cinematic judgment. The day he called in sick, we gave the TV the morning off, too— and we chatted to each other and sipped on instant coffee. I'd do a quick check for everything I'd need for the day— my ID, my spoon, my mug. I was dressed in my only outfit. I had an hour of solitude to groom my eyebrows just right.

You don't see the gates, for the most part. The people who are in charge of your life are clearly marked, and basically abiding by written rules. Sam Rubin speaks to you the same, even though you might never see a movie in a theater again.

Life becomes normal without that IV of freedom jabbing through you. You stop seeing the scar where the needle once pierced.

You just live.

A little more bitter, a lot less heavy.

You aren't free, and that's one less thing you

have to carry.

This morning, I couldn't find the sweater I wanted to wear. My coat didn't fit the one eventually selected, and now the sleeves bunch up inside the other sleeves. I was filled with too much anxiety to even consider breakfast, and the chaos of the outside world didn't slow for even a moment. The people who are in charge of my life here don't wear uniforms. There's no method to their madness. They blend into the fog. There's a thousand smells in the air. A thousand people on the roads. There are a thousand channels on the television, and I don't even know how to use the device. It reminds me that I'm a widow now. He died this year while I was away, and the bittersweet memories fill me. The sweetness thickens my blood, the bitter thickens my skin.

I am heavy, like freedom.
I am free, and sweet.
Sweet and hard.

So easy to crush. So easy to shatter.

Everything in this world comes in hundreds, thousands, and millions.

There are choices on top of choices,
and under them, and behind them.

There's so much to carry in our pockets and purses, and so few moments of stillness to pluck my eyebrows and wonder what Sam Rubin would say.

My mornings start differently now. They're spit-wet lemondrops, slow and sticky, full of small freedoms. The fibers of yesterday cling to the sweet residue of the small stuff I sweat.

It only stings for a second, but that second never stops stinging.
It folds into a minute.

My wound is fresh. I can see the puncture and feel the bruising as gates give way to possibility. I remind myself: sweetness is worth the sting.

I sip my coffee and find KTLA on my phone. I sit by a pond, outside my office, and listen. I remove the coat that doesn't fit, and make a list of the things I have forgotten to carry, and the movies I should go see. There is still too much around me, inside me, behind me, in front of me. But in the temporary peace, I am reminded of the sweetness that can be found in the 59 seconds that don't hurt.

I did 438 days of time, and one little second of pain is nothing in the face of that, even when it's folded into a minute.

Because it's a minute of freedom
and every minute of freedom is so very sweet.

Muscle Memory

Muscles have memory, they say.
I'll be back to fightin' shape in no time.

It's a good habit for muscles to have…
except in those moments where it's an
absolutely
awful
thing.

My muscles remember being shackled.

The little girl across the way plays with a
flashlight.
She is maybe three or four years old,
and it is her favorite toy.
She fearlessly wields the light
that sweeps over her horizon
and laughs in delight
as she magics a pathway
through the darkness.

She is joyful and beautiful.
I am terrified of her.

The ray of her flashlight
enters my house through the front window.
It passes over me and I stop movement.

My muscles remember the command.

I snap my head towards her,
my body perched in readiness.

I slowly process
that I am not being summoned
and I am not being told to freeze.
Consciously,
I lower my shoulders
and shake the stress from my neck.

I take a deep breath,
and everything is fine.

She's just a little girl,
partaking of the freedom
we both now enjoy.

But then she does it again,
and the repetition
doesn't even slightly diminish the response.

She shackles me with her celebration
and my brain is twisting them all together—
the joy of a child's laugh
and the confusion of stunted adrenaline.
She is twisting me up,
twisting me in,
and breaking me down.

My muscles have memory,
and they yield to her light,
giving up their freedom
without slightest fight.

My muscles have memory
and they wake

and bathe and eat
on the schedule of imprisoned women,
a group to which I once belonged.

A group to which I'll belong forever.

You'll be back to fightin' shape in no time,
they say.
But the closest I ever got to fightin' shape
was as property of the state.

My normal shape doesn't fight.
My normal shape melds, spills,
contours and folds.
All my sharpest angles and deepest borders are
products of loss.
Loss of freedom. Loss of love.

My muscles remember my love.

The little girl rises with the sun
and the memory of his death.

They rise to me, and blow me down.
I press his work gloves to my nose.
They are dirty and smell of sweat. Of debris.

My muscles remember, even after all this time.
Even after all this destruction.
They yield to him, and as my shape contours,
I spill over my tallest walls.

My fighting' shape is no match for my lovin'
shape.
I pack away the gloves and wave to the child
across the way.
Her light shines over me.
His light shines in me.

It is painful to remember, but each stab tears
away my angles.
The sharp ones. The dark ones.
I'll be back to lovin' shape in no time,
I comfort myself.
Muscles have memory.

Doing Time

I was delivered to prison, fully-shackled. For the uninitiated, this means there were cuffs on each of my ankles, cuffs on each of my wrists, and a few chains connecting them all together. When you're fully-shackled, you clang and you waddle. It's a funny little side-to-side shuffle that instinctively keeps you balanced... upright... moving forward. Upon arrival, they remove the chains and institutionalize you. It's a different sort of shackle.

I served 438 days, the majority of my incarceration hosted by the state of California's best rehabilitation facilities. I am now in the free world, living under the provisos of probation. It isn't the same as free. It's just a different sort of cage. One with no bars on the windows, just fancy blinds.

This morning, the knocking at the door was determined enough to rattle the window coverings. I guessed it was morning, but I wasn't sure. The twilight of dawn was still set into the sky and I was sleeping.

LA COUNTY PROBATION was shouted through my house so I rushed off the bed and to the door, to present myself. I didn't want them to shake down the whole house. I was still blinking sleep from my eyes.

STEP OUT OF THE HOUSE, they repeated, I don't know how many times. There was 4 or maybe 5 that I could see— fully-armed cops in full gear.

The child stomped behind me and I shushed her back a few feet. There was chaos, a dog, a girl, her dad, my mom, and myself. There was a door, and cops… I wasn't really sure of anything else, but it struck me that I was living my favorite short story— *The Night the Bed Fell*, by James Thurber. Except it was terrifying, and not funny at all.

It was morning, probably, I decided as I was patted down. I faced the car in my driveway as I was cuffed.

"There's a girl inside," I said. "A little girl."

"Is she yours?" they asked.

"No," I said.

They exchanged glances and kept switching off between each other. There were nine, I think.

I hadn't had coffee yet. I wasn't wearing a bra. I was standing in the middle of my street, handcuffed.

My mom stumbled out of the house in her pajamas, propelled by a cop. Her lip was wobbly. Her cheeks were tear-stained.

"Why are you doing this?" she asks, and they explain again.

"It's just a house inspection."

Just.

What a ridiculous word.

I shift so the cuffs aren't visible as the 8-year-old walks out, cuddling her stuffed wolf. She's in her nightgown, too.

I never break eye contact with her, and she's brave with every step. I start babbling about school, and she tells the cop about her Columbus

Day map. I want to look down, to see if they let her put shoes before kicking her out of her house, but I don't want to break eye contact.

After some time, a minute or maybe thirty, they wave everyone back inside and I stand outside with them. They go over the stipulations of my parole. A long list of things of which I have no prior history of entanglement. I promise to not suddenly develop violent tendencies or drug habits or gang affiliations.

I ask where my probation officer is, and they tell me I can call him after. I don't want to sound like a child, but I want him now. This would still have been terrifying, but less so.

They keep saying PROBATION in a near shout, as we talk, and the word echoes down the street. All of my neighbors will know, if they didn't notice my braless-self handcuffed in front of a battalion of police officers.

It doesn't really matter to me, but it might to the people whose house I'm renting. The people who have just had their child dragged from bed. I wonder if I'll be homeless soon, but it's an idle sort of wonderment.

The cop speaking to me seems like a nice lady. She's outraged over my sentence, arguing that a male would have gotten half the time. The male cop claims any Los Angeles resident would have gotten half the time. No matter to me.

I did the time I did.

I wonder if my blankness shows, but it's an idle sort of wonderment.

I think about the women who are not me. The women who don't have friends and family who will be horrified. Who don't live in safe, private neighborhoods. Who don't have good jobs and strong educations. How could they build a life with probation doing everything possible to destroy it?

I wonder, but I don't feel.
I turn when they say turn.
The cuffs come off, but not really.

I hear the clanging of chains when I breathe. It

drowns out the sound of emotion, embarrassment, anger, and fear.

It's morning now, for sure. The light is shining through my cage. The day is striding forward and I shuffle on,

continuing

to

do

time.

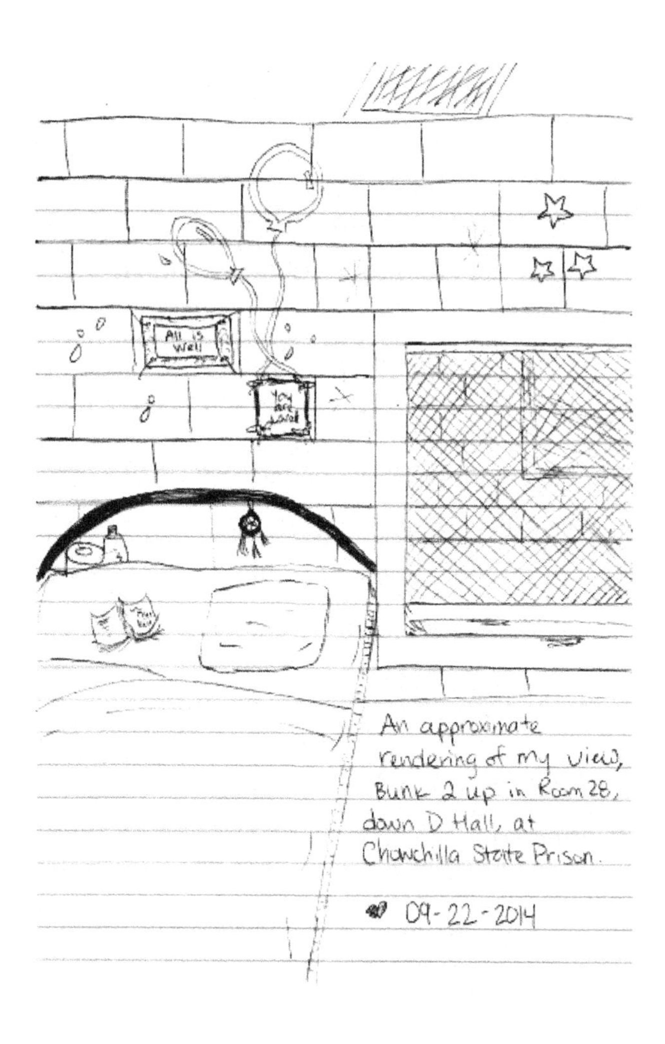

An approximate rendering of my view, Bunk 2 up in Room 28, down D Hall, at Chowchilla State Prison.

09-22-2014

About the Author.

Ra lives and loves in Los Angeles and the Internet, where frightfully wondrous things happen.

She is a once-upon-a-time inmate, a reluctantly-optimistic widow, an exponential storyteller, and also basically a dinosaur. Her own story is a long one— and she's enthusiastically variable in the telling of it— but the short version is she (probably) loves you.

Stop by and say hey:
Rarasaur.com

More titles available:
Hostile17Print.com

Made in the USA
Monee, IL
27 July 2020

37123342R00066